FRIENDS RESURRECT

Tom McMullen
and
Dick Lund

Desideratum*

Herein lies a tale
Outside help for those in need
By connectedness

*de-sid-er-a-tum:
noun
something that is needed or wanted;
something desired as essential

PROLOGUE

This book combines the stories of two friends, Tom McMullen and Dick Lund, both recovering alcoholics. Each of us experienced the throes of life in addiction: stress, loneliness, frustration, anger, shame, anxiety, and hopelessness. Outside help for recovery for both of us inspires us to seek lives rooted in joy, contentment and wisdom of purpose. As such, our new ways of life amount to personal resurrections from living in the depths of life in addiction.

What we attempt to offer here are ways to resurrect the joy of life; to create a life focused on love of others and self; to acquire the wisdom to discover an ever-increasing understanding of our humanity; and to learn the joy and contentment of a spiritually-centered life. We use the 12-Steps of Alcoholics Anonymous as a guide in this process. What we learn is that when we strive to behave in such a way, it is often catching. Our hope is that those who long for a better life will indeed resurrect.

Friends

It's been said that a life without friends is ~~not worth~~ living.
It's also been said it's friends who add enthusiasm to life.

I have a friend

A true friend whom I like and likes me in return.
My friend, who I know well, educes my respect.
A friend who shows love to every one he meets.

I have a friend.

With cheery attitude my friend shows zest for life.
With awe my friend sees wonder of creation.
With reverence my friend sees the hand of God in all.
With gratitude my friend lives life in joy of living.

I have a friend.

By example my friend shows me how to love.
A friend who in so many ways I want to be like.

I have a friend.

— Dick Lund

ABOUT THE AUTHORS

DICK LUND

Permit me to introduce my friend Tom McMullen. Tom lives in the moment, and he finds it generally agreeable. He loves humanity and goes out of his way to show it. By being spiritually centered, he acts out compassion and kindness. His temperament of spontaneity introduces perpetual excitement into his life, and to those around him. Generosity, humility, cheerfulness and a demeanor of gratitude can also be said of him. I've found that just associating with such a person is a humbling experience, and it inspires me to want to be more like him. Of course, as most others in our group would say of Tom, "He's just doing what he's supposed to do." As I hear his stories I imagine Tom, the person in the action, and I find it less than surprising that outcomes are somewhat surreal. At least for me, encounters with Tom resurrect infinite possibilities of new life.

TOM MCMULLEN

Dick Lund is the most inspiring, spiritually informed, spiritually evolved person I've ever met. Dick and I have met every week for 22 years in our AA group, dealing with our alcoholism. Each week he treats our group with his pearls of wisdom. The older he gets, the more frequent and clearer his messages become. Dick is evolving at a rapid rate. In his own words, "It's a mystery."

GROWING UP
WITH DAD

DICK LUND

In growing up, my Dad too, drank a lot,
Abusive, yes, to Mom and kids galore
Improving situation? All for naught.
The same was true his family before.

Dad also taught the virtue of hard work,
His part to pay the bills, as well he should.
Our part to do what's given, not to shirk.
As I see now he did the best he could.

T'was Dad who first showed drink can be abused
For me it happened too while still a teen
Euphoria left mindfulness confused
Addiction took control my very mien.

Now what sort of addicted life takes place?
Beginning young maturity is stalled
Without help insane living runs apace
And unassisted life slows to crawl.

TOM MCMULLEN

My recollection of home life is painful. My father would come home from work, start his cocktail hour, and within the first drink have a personality change. I got the end of his wrath. Family times were not common. My sister Mary Kay got pregnant when she was a junior; I was a sophomore so it was tough around the house. My parents were worried about this happening to my other sisters. My sisters and I had a common foe, so we stuck together.

I developed ulcers by the time I was 13, which really got in my way. By the time I was 19, I had severe stomach troubles and the doctors at the Mayo Clinic wanted to take out part of my stomach. I said no, and entered a six-week hospitalization treatment plan. After two weeks, they wanted me to go into the mental health unit. I agreed to under one condition: that my father would go in with me. The doctors called him and he came down to have a visit with them. They came to me the next day and said, "He decided he wouldn't do it." I wasn't surprised. I knew he wouldn't, and I wasn't going to either. The doctors said that I might as well go home.

I had my first drink of alcohol when I was 13, and then I spent the next 14 years trying to capture that euphoric feeling.

Interestingly, my son TJ was conceived in sobriety and born in September 1971. TJ never witnessed my drinking and the dysfunction it brings. Yet, he had his first beer when he was 13 and was hooked from then on. As of the writing of this book, gratefully, TJ has 20 years of sobriety.

Step 1

> *"We admitted we were powerless
> over alcohol – that our lives
> had become unmanageable."*

Dick Lund

A Remembrance

So what is this? Unmanageable life?
So what's wrong? Bills are paid, the lawn is mowed.
On the other hand, I fight with my wife,
And my boss says get help! My drinking showed.

To begin this road I had to agree
To accept help; thirty-six years ago now.

Out-patient, a sad day of shame for me.
Get better? Confused! I did not know how.

What was there to get? Just tell me the rules.
How does that make you feel? The only cue
The secret part of me that had the tools
To become normal. For me to be new.

Hearing no heart-felt song, Counselor asked,
"Want to be well? In-patient can be had.
Yes! For three more weeks, work a harder task.
As the way to be less lonesome, less sad.

God can help. Seek the way through your trial
To pray, make room for hope, know your soul.
It was new. No comfort in denial,
Getting real. Feel the feeling to be whole.

It was serious. I became involved.
That first step set the way. Kindled the flame.
So many taught us how they evolved.
The message is love, the name of the game.

Treatment, a more abundant way to live;
Hope and joy, a life guided from above.
So much learned, like the power to forgive,
Divine light for true self to do true love.

TOM MCMULLEN

Back before we were married, Trudi wound up getting pregnant with our first daughter. Before that, I could never have made the decision to get married because I was so irresponsible, and drinking a lot. Her friends had warned her that I had a drinking problem, and we would be headed for trouble. She called me and told me she was pregnant and asked, "What should we do?" I replied immediately, "Let's get married." From then on,

I never second-guessed that decision! Trudi and I were married on June 4, 1966. It was a rainy day. We had so much fun together. Her family was our life and they accepted me.

Her family also saw my drinking. I created so many bad situations because I became boisterous and belligerent when I drank. I went through a party stage, but you could count on the fact that by the end of the night I would become snarly and get ugly. Trudi's dad tried to get me out of the bar one night and I wouldn't leave. Trudi said, "Why didn't you bring him home with you?" He said, "You go try and get him out of that bar." One time I was just so drunk, I fell into a mud puddle on the family farm right in front of Trudi and her mother. They still accepted me because Trudi did. I was exciting to Trudi – she didn't want farm life. For her, it was stifling. She always told me, "When you walk into a room, you have so much confidence, and when I walk into a room, I have none." She liked my flair! When we were going together, Trudi wasn't always around when I was drinking heavily. I would drop her off at night and go off to drink. She didn't know how bad my drinking was until after we got married, and actually neither did I.

Trudi at first didn't think I was an alcoholic, but eventually she realized I was. My compulsive drinking caused an awful lot of pain. After I joined AA for the second time, Trudi really embraced it. She came to the meetings with me and would sit off to the side with the spouses while the alcoholics would have their meeting. Afterwards, on the way home, Trudi would say, "Gee, it was so interesting, Tom, when they said something about what alcoholics do." I would tell them that I didn't do any of those things, but she'd bring up examples of how I did. I realized that I was deluded; I had either forgotten or minimized those incidences. It was so great for me having Trudi in that room giving me feedback. She sat in with me for about two months and then helped start a group for spouses of alcoholics. She grabbed a hold of and lived the Al-Anon program.

Step 2

"Came to believe that a Power greater than ourselves could restore us to sanity."

Dick Lund

The Mystery of Grace

The things we do are often called insane,
For most of us, like me, self will's the bane.
Protecting self by casting truth aside,
A habit grows by yielding to our pride.

A better way came knocking at my door,
A way of being, with power to restore.

I listened, what I heard came to my soul.—
A feeling like a love that made me whole.

It came to me to act a different way,
To grow the feeling, meditate and pray.
That love suffused in life is sanity,
A joyful and contented way to be.

From whence belief that God can ease our bane,
Bestow this gift of feeling we are sane?
Slow to see, but convinced of some grand scheme.
I did see others changed, and were redeemed.

Sanity restored; given by God's grace.
A light divine illuminates our pace,
In life-long walk with our Lord side by side.
God's mystery of soul and grace abide.

TOM MCMULLEN

The University of Minnesota's Engineering Office is where I met Trudi. I was working in construction and was all dirty and grubby when I walked in to register. She registered me. Trudi had been raised in Alden, MN and had attended Mankato State for one year, but transferred to the U of M. I just thought she was the coolest thing. I asked her for her phone number and she gave it to me. I went home and told my sister Marcy, "I just met the girl I'm going to marry." Right from the start I was turned-on by her!

I waited a couple of days and called her to see if she'd go out with me. She said, "I have this boyfriend now but he goes back to Mankato in a couple weeks. So, why don't you call me after that?" I was crushed! My ego was bruised, of course, and I didn't call her. But she had my class schedule and after about a week, she started appearing outside my classrooms, pinning something up on the bulletin boards. I would say "Hi" to her all the time and she'd just kind of pretend I wasn't there. One day, after a week of this sparring, she turned around and looked me straight in the eye and said "Hi" back. We went together from then on.

Trudi was really attractive and I remember she was just easy to be with. We went to a movie on the first date. When she got out of the car and walked down the street, I asked, "Are you limping?" She said, "Yeah, I had polio when I was young, and my left leg is affected a little bit." Of course, I was more endeared to her than before because my sister Cathy had polio. It was not negative that Trudi limped; I looked at it as a positive! She was just different from the wife I had pictured for myself – I had pictured someone like my sister, Marcy who is meek, quiet, and in the background. Trudi was just a handful!

Little did we know what was in store for us in the coming years.

Fast-forwarding several years, which will be accounted for as you read on, I met Pat at Fairview Hospital. My sisters and I were there to be with my mother while she had some tests. She was going to be in an exam for about an hour so I thought I would look up a friend who just started a new chemical dependency (CD) counseling job with the hospital. I went to the front desk and was told that CD was on the seventh floor. When I got to the floor there was only a "Mental Health" sign. I asked, "Where's CD?" The lady behind the glass window said they hadn't had CD there for seven years. I said, "Well, your front desk doesn't know it." I told her who I was looking for, and she and another lady gave me phone numbers of other Fairview locations. We had some fun interaction, and I finally reached the voicemail of my counselor friend.

As I was leaving, I stopped myself and said, "You chicken, you were attracted to that lady and if you don't go back and say something you're going to regret it." So, I went back to the window and pointed to Pat and said, "Would you come out here and give me one minute of your time?" She said, "Sure," and came out and stood right in front of me. I said, "I was attracted to you and noticed you weren't wearing a wedding ring. I'm a widower and if you are available I'd like to ...." And kind of ran out of words. I said, "I knew what to say to get you out here, but now I don't know what to say."

Her name was Pat and she took over. She asked me where I lived. When I told her I lived on the south side of Dred Scot Field, she said she lived in the outdated townhouses on the north side of the field. She gave me her phone number and I said I would call when I returned from my two-week trip to Brazil. I waited two days and called her. I just wanted her to know that I was sincere about seeing her when I returned. She said that she had thought even if I didn't call her, she was thrilled to have had the highly charged interaction that we both seemed to have had.

I came back from Brazil four days early. I told Pat there were three reasons. 1.) My mother almost died, 2.) I had a number of very important business things happening, and 3.) I had met this woman whom I couldn't get off my mind. Which one do you think was my motivator?

Our first date was a simple Friday night for a very informal dinner. Pat told me she was leaving for Florida on Sunday, staying till Thursday. I was already lonesome for her before she left. Her Florida friends said she kept asking, "Is it Thursday yet?"

Our next date was a Saturday drive down the Mississippi River to Lake City to watch the eagles. I drove up to her house and she came out carrying a bag of goodies. She had peanuts and bananas and crackers and cheese. I reached in the back seat and opened my bag – peanuts and bananas and crackers and cheese. It was then that I knew that we might have something special going on between us.

Pat and I were married a year later, March 17, 2006. Pat says she enjoys the product that Trudi helped hone.

STEP 3

"Made a decision to turn our will and our lives over to the care of God as we understood Him."

DICK LUND

God is a Mystery

I'm baffled e'en to first begin this poem,
Perplexity encountered with Step One,
When unclear thoughts swirled in my troubled mind,
And answers to God's questions there were none.

May well be said my entire state of mind
Sad attitude and outlook life in grief

No matters of my soul could comprehend
No hope in store nor visions of relief.

But working through step one my outlook cleared,
Though lack of Godly feelings still held sway.
The progress I was making gave me cheer,
Change going on, I'm like the potter's clay.

My mind has rightly cleared in many ways,
Enough to live a life with seeds to sow.
Bewildered in accepting God always,
Mindful that of God I'll never know.

The Step Three promise of the care of God
Begs no issue that we must understand.
A mystery's what we're given, us be awed,
Abides with us today; life, ain't that grand?

TOM MCMULLEN

Between Christmas and New Years in 1969, my sister Mary Kay, had heard a high school friend of mine, Patrick, speak at the New Hope Alano Club. Mary Kay went with her husband Larry to his AA meetings there. She called me, told me about Patrick speaking, and said, "If Patrick can stop drinking, you can stop." She said she asked him to call me.

Patrick called on New Years Eve day, which is my birthday. He invited me to come to his Normandale Group's AA New Years Eve party. I told him, "No, I'm having a party at my house and I won't be coming, thanks." And we hung up.

Probably less than an hour later he called again and asked, "Did you change your mind and decide to come to our New Years Eve party?" And I said, "No." We small talked and hung up.

Then an hour later he called a third time and I declined him again.

An hour later the phone rang again and the fellow on the other end said, "Tom?" And I cut him off abruptly saying, "What do you want me to do? Call everyone I invited and tell them I'm not having my New Years Eve party? That I'm going to some AA party instead?!" And the caller said, "Tom, this is Tim." It was my brother in law. In those days, my parties were mostly with family. So I said, "Tim, you heard me say that. Would you call everyone and tell them I'm canceling and that I'm going to an AA New Years Eve party?" He said he would, and Trudi and I went to Patrick's party that night.

For the next two weeks, I attended Thursday night AA meetings at the Normandale Group, but drank again on January 12th. I went back to the meeting the following week, and as of the writing of this book I have 44 years of sobriety.

STEP 4

"Made a searching and fearless moral inventory of ourselves."

DICK LUND

Life Then and Now

As I reflect on lesson for tonight,
What comes to mind is seeing how I was
And what became of me since first I knew
To gather self together in clear sight.

Back when step four, its words hung on the wall,
Bade ill for me to overcome my fear,
To muster courage needed to respond,
To sketch my portrait true with warts and all.

Confession then and goodness for my soul
Showed themselves as mysteries hand in hand.
The moral side of me was life enriched,
To separate myself did take its toll.

In search of soul each day I now pursue
For ways I can become a better me.
To live as one both human and divine
And share whatever grace God may imbue.

TOM MCMULLEN

After three months of my sobriety, Trudi made an appointment at the Johnson Institute, a place where alcoholics and their families could get counseling. We went for our appointment and the counselor told us to say something good about each other. "What do you think is good about Trudi?" I said a number of things: a good mother, etc. When it was Trudi's turn, he asked her, "Can you say one good thing about Tom, or one thing you like about him?" Trudi thought for a while, put her head down, started crying and said, "I can't think of anything good to say about Tom." That was the start of our rebuilding our life together. Trudi and I began going to an Encounter group there. We went every week for almost a year.

Of course, I was on the hot seat a lot in the group because I was a mouthy guy. Some might have thought that the people there were hard-nosed, mean, tough, and punishing. But I took it as nothing but love. These people loved me and were trying to help me. I was a hard case. It took me six months to absorb this one lesson: "You're feeling guilty because of what you did, not because of Trudi bringing it up to you. You just took it out on her." They had been telling me that for what seemed like ten times a night for six months. Actually hearing that and owning it changed my life. Since that moment, I have never blamed anyone else for my situation. If something is not right with me, I know that it is up to me to make the necessary changes to fix it. That was the start of our rebuilding our life together.

Trudi and I put on a couples' hybrid AA/Encounter group meeting on Friday nights. We had a lot of couples come and great things would happen! During that year, we went to marriage counseling. Our first marriage counselor was Fred Kiel. Fred liked us both and was great for us. He gave us specific things to do. For example, we had to earn points every day. I'd earn a couple points if I'd call home during the day and let Trudi know I was thinking about her. If I helped her with the kids that night, helped with the dishes, or said, "You go out tonight and have some time for yourself, I'll take care of the kids," I'd earn points. I had to earn 35 points a day in order for her to have a good day. I had eight or nine things I had to do. Trudi also had to earn 35 points a day. She had to do two things: one worth 18 and the other worth 17. She had to not bitch, pick, or criticize me all day, and say one good thing about me. Throughout our marriage, we always resorted back to "points" to get us back on track. We also learned that there are only six basic feelings: mad, sad, glad, ashamed, hurt, and scared. Every other feeling is just an offshoot of one of these.

When Trudi was 32 and I was 33, she was diagnosed with a spinal tumor. It was just devastating. The doctors at the Mayo Clinic had hoped it might be a cyst and they could just peel it out of her spinal canal. She had the surgery while our mothers and I waited. When the pathologist came to give us the diagnosis, he had his hands in his pockets. He looked at me and said, "It wasn't a cyst and this is not good news." They couldn't take the tumor out, but they made room for it to expand. It was expected that she wouldn't live long. They told us to go home and have a good Christmas. That was in September! Trudi spent more than a month in the hospital and came home so weak and discouraged. I had to care for our three kids and for Trudi. She was trying to recover from the terrible back surgery, all of the radiation, and the mental stress of not knowing if she was going to live.

One day, Trudi got off the couch, came into the kitchen and said, "Tom, it just hit me: I may not die from this anytime soon. This may be the best I feel for the rest of my life. I'm not going to waste another moment!" From that moment on, Trudi was transformed. She spent the next 25 years in moment-to-moment living. She decided that she was going to live as if this moment was all she had! I had six years of sobriety at the time. I was so grateful for that and for all the work we had done together, because Trudi got to see that I was committed to the family and to her. She taught me how to live in the moment as well.

Over the years that Trudi was in a wheelchair she would go through various stages of losing physical abilities, and that signaled a time for the family to get together to process – to talk, cry, accept and pray – and within a day or two, turn the light back on and get on with our daily lives. During one of these times Trudi was at the kitchen table when a cardinal landed on the birdfeeder, inches away from the window, and stared right at Trudi. She said, "Tom, I feel like that's the Holy Spirit just coming with a message for me. I just know I'm going to be all right!" Since that time, a cardinal has always been special in Trudi's life and our family's.

Step 5

*"Admitted to God, to ourselves,
and to another human being
the exact nature of our wrongs."*

Dick Lund

Second Nature Through Step Five

Recall your life when you first took step five?
What did you find of joy to be alive?
You're there to learn what new life has to teach
But power to learn as yet was out of reach.

You work to put an end to guilt and shame
Excuses will not do, they are so lame.

Speak honestly, you're told, speak from your heart;
A liberating habit from the start.

Confessing wrongs, so hard, to God and friend,
Must then be done to put life on the mend.
The wrongs you did you'll never more repeat,
A vow you made unmindful you can't meet.

Your work goes on, Grace visits, you forgive,
You learn you're not the person you once lived.
You changed, you know not how, your mind has cleared.
You're god's creature now, and one to be revered.

Step five in all it's turmoil, now past.
Your early fear of it was not to last.
You now see light on truth of who you are,
Reminding us God's care abides not far.

New outlook, then, emerging as you hear
Your loving God expressed by brothers dear.
Step Five has shown a road to tread each day,
You've grown to love each step along the way.

TOM McMULLEN

I continued going to AA meetings at the Normandale Group. Chuck took me aside every week and said, "Tom, you said this…" and he'd repeat what had I said. But then he would give me another way to look at the situation. He'd give me a healthy outlook on what I said and show me a healthy way to react. He'd tell me to try thinking that new way in the coming week. He also told me that the words I used were so important and that they would shape my character. I would say, "I should do such-and-such." And he would tell me that another way to say that is "I intend to," or "it might helpful to". This new way of speaking helped me take pressure off myself. He was such a blessing. He had nine years of sobriety at the time, and he gave me all of his wisdom – just pumped it right into my head. Chuck had such a profound influence on my life!

In her own way, Trudi helped to reinforce what Chuck had been teaching me. If I was mad or upset at the kids, she would say, "Tom, consider this other aspect." Or even, "Tom, maybe it could be your own issues that are influencing you."

Before she died, Trudi said two things to me as far as advice. One was, "Your job is to be a consultant or advisor for the family, not a director." The other was, "Don't offer your advice unless you're asked." These have been a work in process for me, and evolving.

I've been going to a chiropractor twice a week for two years. Cassie has worked there for about a year and a half. She is a young lady with much potential, enthusiasm, energy, she's just so bright. And early on she used a lot of self-defeating words. "I should do this." "I need to do this." I've learned that those kinds of statements really short circuit personal growth.

I did with her what Chuck did with me when I first started AA. I told her there might be a better way to say things; that she could choose different words. Then I gave Cassie the Wayne Dyer CDs, "There's a Spiritual Solution to Every Problem." She listens to them on her 40-minute commute to and from work. Often we talked about things Wayne had said and how impactful they were to Cassie. It has been such a rewarding experience to see how she has changed. The confidence that she has, the way she thinks, and how she passes it along to others.

About three months ago, she gave the CDs to her coworker, Emily. Something wonderful happened at my recent appointment. Cassie just couldn't wait to tell me what a profound impact those CDs have had on Emily. And the one part that was especially influential to her is where Wayne says, "If you knew who walked beside you at all times, on the path that you have chosen, you could never experience fear or doubt again." How wonderful for a young lady to be comforted by this so early in life.

STEP 6

"Were entirely ready to have God remove all these defects of character."

TOM MCMULLEN

I see beauty in the faces of people I meet as I go about my day. I'm surrounded by people who are willing to tell a little part of their story, who are kind, ordinary and are struggling through life. I wrote a poem about what I think when I meet a stranger:

> *Hassled and hurried you seem not to care*
> *It probably only registered that I had no hair*
>
> *I love you and of myself I will give*
> *What a blessed life I've been allowed to live!*

I used to think I was important you know,
And things weren't right if I wasn't running the show

I felt pressure, pain, anger and fear
Words of wisdom I was too blocked to hear.

What happened and what I'm like now
Is really a miracle, holy cow!

That I can love and think of you first
Is what I'm about, and my spiritual thirst.

I know in my heart I'm led the right way
Although I was tested when there was no pay.

Day by day, hour by hour
I'm blossoming-what a beautiful flower!

There is some wilt every now and then
But I appreciate even that from where I've been.

Hello? I say to the stranger I meet
Despite your foibles, I think you're neat.

If I were the Creator, you in my hand I would hold
And because of your flaws, on you I'd be sold!

Your turn will come to hold me, hooray!
And then you won't notice my crooked toupee.

DICK LUND

About two years ago, my wife Mary and I began a life-changing habit of Candle Time. This is an early-morning pursuit, occupation, avocation, habit, work, endeavor and/or calling.

During this time we discuss life experiences of the previous day; how we felt about them, the positives, the negatives, what we learned about them, about each other, what could have been better, and how. We share joys and gratitudes. We also take turns reading through a formative book. We are nearly finished, at this writing, with a book Tom McMullen gave us. Tom himself, a wounded healer, gave us a copy of *Mind Whispering*, by Tara Bennett-Goleman. Last summer, Tara gave a seminar at the University of Minnesota Center of Spirituality, which Tom attended and bought a copy of the book for me. *Mind Whispering* is one of the most helpful books I have read.

The subtitle of the book is "A New Map To Freedom From Self-Defeating Emotional Habits." Tara bases the book on three philosophies: Buddhism, Cognitive Therapy, and Horse Whispering. She entwines three thoughts of Buddhist philosophy, which she calls modes, having to do with our conscious awareness of attraction, avoidance, and bewilderment.

Cognitive therapy, I've since learned, is the standard for treating alcohol addiction. It was applied to me in group therapy re-habilitation 36 years ago.

Tara uses Horse Whispering to illustrate how to understand the modes we are in as well as the modes others are in, so that we can change our outlooks and sentiments for the better, in order to attain a "Lightness of Being."

As Mary and I have our Candle Time conversations on this book, we are both amazed at how well it has led us into discovering and diminishing our own "Self-Defeating Emotional Habits."

Our Candle Time came about from a sermon at church. All of us were given a small sack with a candle and a scripture verse, and a suggestion to offer each other a blessing. For Mary and me it evolved into witness from the heart – and growing love for one another.

As we have delved into *Mind Whispering*, we've learned much more about ourselves and each other. Conflict is nearly ended. Tara left us with two mantras: first, pay attention to intention; second, be aware of awareness.

STEP 7

*"Humbly asked Him to
remove our shortcomings."*

DICK LUND

A Visitation of Grace

*An inventory of the way I was
Not pretty, but will always keep in mind.
Walked the dark side past, wreckage left behind
Crossed to the light side, Grace to give me pause.*

*It began with God within me, thanks to Doug
Who chanced to mention God he understood.
The feeling caught me, feeling that I could
Learn respect with love as child of God*

As child of God came feeling self up-lift,
To share redemption which we're all a part.
Now God must be life-giving in my heart
From love the feeling comes of Spirit's gifts.

These gifts I never felt nor came to dwell.
Compassion, joy, control of self and more,
New way of life, new images, new lore.
Foretaste of life to come I can't foretell.

This inventory who I am today
Needs daily tote of wealth stored in my soul,
To scatter, lending purpose, makes me whole.
God beckoned me to change; my "yes" held sway.

Tom McMullen

I found hope in my AA program. We went through a time in our life where we were so incredibly broke. Once I went two and a half years without making a dime. I used to drive to the airport and park in valet, walk in, buy a McDonald's coffee, sit down and watch people go by. I was at my wit's end and was so lost. I'd look at those people and just think, "Okay, as soon as things get turned around, we're going to be out here taking trips again." That was my weekly therapy session and how I could get up in the morning, go to work, not make any money, all the while believing that success was just around the corner. I just knew that the next call I made would be The One, if I would just keep at it. I borrowed money from friends, maxed out many credit cards, and didn't pay the IRS. I went into a deep financial hole. Finally my tenacity paid off! Within three years, we turned it around, paid back every dime, and wound up at a point where Trudi was able to say, "I can't believe how good things are."

My business life totally changed. Although outwardly it might have seemed that I operated pretty much like always. I used to think subconsciously that if someone had to lose in a deal it would be me. And I would think that someone would notice just how valuable I was and pay me accordingly. It didn't happen. Now I realize that we are all in this together to make something good happen, and we will share in the payout appropriately. I used to use my abundant energy to drag a deal across the finish line. To say the least, it's tough on the one who thinks they must supply all the energy. I remember the moment when I decided to change this. It was like an awakening. I decided that if I wasn't "pulled" into a deal, I was going to pass on the opportunity. I wasn't going to try to force things to happen. I remember my phone ringing about five minutes later. I looked at the phone and said to myself, "Things are different now." The caller said, "Tom, we need your help." At that moment, I felt the presence of a Divine Power in my life and I knew I was beginning a new, great journey.

Kevin was referred to me because he wanted to buy a company. My business has been mergers and acquisitions; helping buyers and sellers of companies get together. Kevin didn't have much money, and he was not what I had in mind as a model of a hard-charging entrepreneur, like so many I had worked with in the past. Kevin did have something that mysteriously drew me to him and that made me want to go all out for him. A couple of months later, I found him and his two partners a perfect deal. They ran that business successfully for eight to ten years, and I stayed close to Kevin. I was happy for him, and thankful that I had gone with my intuition about him. Eventually, however, he was forced out of the business by his partners. He had pretty much lost everything because of the way things ended. Six months later, he called me looking for a job. I told him that I could find him a job, but I thought he should buy another company, this time without partners. About five months later, he was the proud owner of a very successful manufacturing company. He's made money every year, even in the major recession that our country experienced.

That's the background, but here's the real story. About three years ago, Kevin called me and told me his wife, Cindy, was in the emergency room at North Memorial Hospital. He said he knew she was dying and couldn't get anyone to take any action. He'd done everything he could and was now calling for my help. I told him I would do something. "Let's get off the phone," I said. I immediately called North Memorial and asked for Dr. David Lilja, who was head of the emergency/EMT department. He wasn't in, neither was his assistant. The only one around was the young lady in the department who answered the phone. I told her of the situation and said that it was up to her whether Cindy lived or died. She said she would do something.

Kevin called me an hour and a half later and said, "I don't know what you did, but just minutes after we hung up, doctors were rushing into Cindy's room." She was taken for immediate surgery, nearly dead from internal bleeding.

I have never asked Kevin why he called me at that moment. He had no idea that I had any dealings with Dr. Lilja. But, we're all connected. I think events are all connected. Twenty-five years earlier I had met Dr. Lilja while working on a product I was trying to develop. In 1982, Tony Coniglario, age 45, and former major league baseball star, had a heart attack. While en route to the hospital the EMTs performed CPR on Tony, but had trouble doing it properly. I read that news story and thought, "I can develop a fool-proof CPR device." I met Dr. Lilja at that time. The device never worked, but Cindy and Kevin know that something else was working here. Tony Conglario's crisis was an inspiration for giving Cindy life.

Pat and I went to Jacksonville, FL for my nephew's wedding. After checking into our hotel, we drove a couple of miles to a grocery store to buy goodies to eat during our stay. At the store, we noticed a young mother with a son about five years old and a toddler who was riding the grocery cart. The young boy was so loving and nice and spirited with his little sister. The mother was that way with both of them. Pat and I talked about how inspiring it was to watch their interaction. They were checking out in front of us. When their grocery tab was totaled, the mother reached into her wallet for all of her cash, $10-15, and three credit cards in order to get enough to pay her $50-60 bill. I immediately spoke up and said, "The groceries are on us. We've been watching you as we shopped and were moved by the fun spirit and love all of you show for each other." She accepted graciously and went on her way. The next night we went out with my sisters and other family members who had come for the wedding. My sister Cathy had to scramble to find a restaurant that could accommodate all of us at a table. She was able to get reservations within walking distance from our hotel. After we were seated a lady came by and was filling our water glasses when I noticed her and Pat reacting to each other. "You're the people from the grocery store," the server said. Tears were shed and wonderful words exchanged. Turns out that that was her first night working there and her husband was home with the kids. We are often moved by our memories of that inspiring moment.

STEP 8

"Made a list of all persons we had harmed, and became willing to make amends to them all."

DICK LUND

Apology Then Amends

Who wants to face old friends?
Admit, then make amends?
Regretful, yet seeking release,
From guilt that will not cease.

Just why from this we shrink?
Pride clouds the ways we think.

Our blindness did no harms reveal.
Now see, begin to heal.

A frightful thing at best,
But get it off your chest.
At first this step helps only you;
"I'm sorry" must make do.

Much later you will find
Amends of deeper kind.
To act the life you will create,
From soul with grace innate.

What changes will you make?
Your choice, for your own sake.
Honest, friendly, disciplined too;
Happiness is your due.

Empathic and contrite,
Discerning all that's right.
Making the habit to be kind,
Humble with peace of mind.

New self now settled in.
Amend so genuine,
Shows life abounding graciously.
Love abides, three times three.

TOM MCMULLEN

I admired the way she was. Trudi gave more than her share in our marriage, especially in the early years. She was the one accountable for things. She organized the family and kept our lives together. I got to make up for that later on.

A couple years after her surgery, Trudi started using a cane. I remember when I bought the cane for her. The tumor was expanding and filling the cavity in her spine, so she started tripping. I bought the prettiest cane I could find, came home, and placed the it on the railing. Trudi saw me, the cane, and never said a word. We didn't talk about it for two days, but then she started to use it around the house. She said, "When you brought that cane home, I was so mad, but I knew I needed it, and am grateful."

After about five years with the cane, Trudi was becoming very unsure of herself, so I started to look at wheelchairs. I came home one day and told her, "Trudi, I found a wheelchair and put it in the garage in case you ever need it." Oh, she was ticked! A few nights later, she was washing dishes and went to back up. I was in the family room, heard a crash, and ran into the kitchen. Here was this beautiful woman lying on her back with blood all over her. Her upper body had gone backwards but her feet did not move, and she sliced her head open on a cupboard handle. In the car on the way to the hospital, we laughed and cried. Trudi said what she would often say, "What a mess I've gotten you into! Isn't this something?" I responded, "What you have gotten me into is a blessing. I'm honored to be with you. I get to live my life with you."

Our kids have had good teachers in resiliency. They've seen some really significant things. When TJ went through treatment the second time, he was told, "TJ, you know how to live a sober life. It's been modeled to you for 24 years."

STEP 9

"Made direct amends to such people wherever possible, except when to do so would injure them or others."

DICK LUND

Forgiveness

There was a time, in days gone by,
When getting well, was not yet nigh.

I had not felt God touch my soul,
Nor could I feel a self, made whole.

I asked of God my fear erase,
To meet those wronged then, face to face.

So self endured, learned through God's grace,
My self to love, no fear deface.

To make amends, God's gift is near,
The power of love, to quell our fear.

You're not so bad, don't worry so.
You made mistakes, some time ago.

You've made your list, your thoughts rehearsed,
Amends, amends, your loved ones first.

Telling the truth of days gone by,
Settles your soul, a restful sigh.

What harm you did, they will forgive.
Those days have passed, love as you live.

TOM McMULLEN

I don't remember much about my father in my younger years. One time he walked with me to Buck's Drug Store and another time played catch with me in the backyard. The greatest memory is when he took me pheasant hunting for the first time when I was five. It was Thanksgiving Day, and he and my Uncle Hank went road hunting while I sat in the back seat of the car. We went out by Shakopee along the Minnesota River; we were riding along and I said, "I saw a duck, I saw a duck!" Hank said, "Naw, there was nothing there, I didn't see anything." My father kept driving while I kept saying, "I saw a duck, I saw a duck!" And Hank kept saying, "Naw, there was nothing there." Finally, my dad asked what the duck looked like. "It had a white ring around its neck!" My dad hit the brakes, turned around, and went back to where I had seen it. He got out, loaded his gun and I told him it was over by a post. So, he walked up to the post and this great big pheasant flew up! He shot it and it landed in the river. We followed that bird for most of the afternoon until my father got a boater's attention to bring it to us.

In the wintertime, I speed skated, and was pretty good. The finals were sponsored by the City of Minneapolis and were at Powderhorn Park. My father came to watch me. He gave me some advice before the race started, and we both ended up wishing he hadn't. He said, "Don't start out very fast, let these guys get ahead of you. Then, when they all get burned out, make your move." Well, I let them get almost half a rink ahead of me before I made my move and just ran out of time. I realized afterwards I could have sprinted the entire race and won easily. I had the stamina and drive that was great in competition, but my dad didn't know that! He probably meant for me to stay close to them, but I took him literally.

After my father died, at the age of 85, my mother, who was 81, moved to a very "upbeat" senior living residence. She developed a group of friends who were always together. My mother was the ringleader. She'd organize trips to the racetrack, downtown for plays, happy hours at restaurants, anywhere they could go and have fun. They dined every night together. How my mom loved her meals. She said living there was like living in a five star hotel, only with sorority sisters. She was very healthy and active. She drove all over town and never missed a family party or get together. (She wouldn't give her friends rides because she didn't want to get sucked into being a taxi driver.)

A visit to the dermatologist showed a little trouble spot on her face. Turned out to be a very aggressive cancer called Merkel Cell Cancer. It was then I had a little visit with my father. I said to him, "you haven't been the easiest person to live with over the years." (I used much stronger language.) "You have a chance to make up for all of that. I want you to make sure Mom has a quick, painless, peaceful death."

Nine days before she died, she was driving around town visiting people. She had one half night in the hospice and died. She never missed a meal, even the day of her death, November 18, 2005. She was happy, healthy, and then dead.

Thank you, Dad. If there was left over resentment or blame, it's all over and forgiven, with love.

Pat likes church and I go with her. Without my "wanting to be with her," church isn't something I'd do. On February 15, 2013, the minister said something about asking forgiveness for our wrongs, and then to pray for any special intention. In this particular situation, I thought about the polarization that my son holds for me, and contemplated what my role was in that, and I thought of his deceased mother who was so loving and accepting toward him — and him towards her. I asked her to help. I did this by visualizing a bright white light flowing. It started with Trudi and then to TJ and then to me. It permeated and illuminated our bodies until we were completely pure, and then united, the three of us. Peace came over me and I knew things were going to be all right between us. I opened my eyes to hear the choir singing. About 20 seconds into my listening, I was startled and comforted by one of the ladies whose singing sounded like Ann Murray. I leaned to Pat and said, she sounds just like Ann Murray. Then it hit me, before I finished the sentence – Ann Murray was Trudi's favorite singer and Trudi was giving me a sign that she was there to help.

STEP 10

"Continued to take personal inventory and when we were wrong promptly admitted it."

DICK LUND

A Walk in the Light

For those of us who've slowed down with this part
Think not you're safe to let time slip away,
Admit your wrongs, be honest from the start,
Look in the mirror, and see your feet of clay.

Admitting to another, hard indeed,
Words from your heart of wrongs that you regret.

Preparing well, your talk, your ear in need,
Of kind remarks, and how you pay your debt.

The pain you feel to tell the way you were,
Your time with God, release your guilt with peace
Catharsis for your soul, your conscience stirred.
Bad habits left behind, bad feelings cease.

Your AA life is ready to proceed,
Confronting self of ways you used to be.
New insights heard from others meet your need,
Forgiving self and learning to be free.

TOM McMULLEN

The most difficult time of our lives was ten months before Trudi died. Doctors told her that due to all the radiation she received 25 years earlier, she had developed an aggressive Lymphoma that was one step away from being untreatable. The only way to beat it was a bone marrow transplant, and to have this procedure, she needed chemo to get the Lymphoma in remission. The odds were so small. None of us tried to influence Trudi in her decision. She made the decision to go for it. Everyone quit what they were doing – TJ ultimately lost his job because of his commitment to his mother. Melissa's employer wanted her to do more, but she said that she would be doing less. She wound up leaving. Melanie had a chance to get out of her job and receive a severance. Both daughters delayed their weddings. I immediately stopped everything I was doing and moved my office to my house. I knew where my focus needed to be and spent the next ten months in moment-to-moment living.

Trudi's goal was to beat the Lymphoma. For ten months we were together as a family in Rochester where Trudi received chemo and got the stem cell transplant. We rented two apartments for our kids, their significant others, grandson, and dogs. We'd watched Dr. Phil and Oprah, while Trudi got her chemo. After watching Oprah everyday, I used to think all businesses should shut down for one hour and watch her show. What a softening effect it would have on the world. We got through this the same way we got through the other 25 years of her illness. Every time something difficult would happen, we'd come together, cry, hold and love each other, and pray until we all were ready to go on. We did that until Trudi was successfully discharged from the bone marrow transplant on a Friday afternoon. She was so excited! She called TJ as were leaving and she said, "Hey, I'm going home!"

Over the weekend it became apparent that something was not right and we went back to Rochester on Monday morning. She was admitted, had more tests and found out on Thursday that the lymphoma had come back. Her life span was now measured in weeks. The doctors at Rochester helped get her body stabilized so that she could go home. On Saturday, her primary doctor came in to express his sadness over her lymphoma. Trudi was so shocked! On Thursday she hadn't really heard what the doctors had told her, so on Saturday it really hit home. As we were pulling out of town, she said, "Tom, I want your attention. I want you to know I'm not going home to die. I'm going to live my life that same way I've been living it for the last 25 years. I'm not going to live in fear, pain and worry. I'm going to take advantage of every moment, so let's go."

I hurt my back helping Trudi out of the van the first day she was home. Melanie moved into our house and took charge of Trudi's care. Melissa had become pregnant during Trudi's treatments and because of the chemo, Melissa could not help with Trudi's care. Back at the hospital, Melanie had learned from the physical therapist and nurses how to work with Trudi once she came home. She gave Trudi perfect, round-the-clock, gentle loving care for three weeks. She is so much like Trudi in so many ways. They had so many precious moments together during that time.

Throughout her treatment, Trudi took pain medication only twice. The night before she died, I put a drop of medication on her tongue to help her throat relax and in the morning I did it again to help her speak. She used to say, "You have to manage the pain, you can't let the pain manage you." The morning of her death was a profound spiritual experience. Trudi had vomited a little bit during the night. I called the hospice lady to tell her about it. She said that if there was anyone you want to be with Trudi when she dies, tell them to get on the move because in the next 24 hours, Trudi was probably going to die. I called her brother and mother who were up in Alexandria. TJ and his wife, Caroline, and little Tommy, had been staying with us, but Trudi had asked them to go home the previous night because Tommy had been fussy and everyone needed a good night's sleep. I called TJ and told him what the hospice lady had said and to plan on coming over later. He was packing, and said he would be over later on. I went back to the bedroom, took a look at Trudi and noticed things had changed in the few minutes I had been out of the room. I called TJ and said, "Don't waste time. Come right now." I thank God for the little voice that led me to make that call. TJ and his family got there 20 minutes later and he had 45 minutes with his mom before she died.

Trudi died February 5th, 2002 at 11:11 a.m. Trudi wasn't able to speak for about an hour before her death. In her last minutes, she said plainly to our kids who were holding her hands, "Lift up my arms." Then she said, "Okay," and they put her arms down. The last word she said, with her last breath was, "Tom." We were all together on the bed with her. Melanie noted then that it was 11:11, which was a Trudi-type thing to notice. Her brother, mother and sister-in-law Colleen showed up about an hour later. We kept Trudi at our house a good part of the day. The hospice lady came later and I told her about the experience we had at Trudi's death. She said, "Many times, people who have lived near-death experiences report having had this vision of people reaching out to them." We think that when Trudi asked us to lift up her arms, it was because loved ones were saying to her, "Come with us Trudi."

During the ten months before Trudi's death, I never once contemplated her dying. All I thought was what our children and I could do to help her beat this cancer. I absolutely lived in the moment and felt blessed to have been given what we all were given, to experience this in an almost perfect way.

I'm humbled by the journey Trudi and I took together. What started with Trudi putting her head down and crying years earlier when she couldn't think of one good thing to say about me, to her last word being, "Tom." I consider that Trudi spoke my name and it was heard in heaven. This knowing has had a very profound affect on my life. Thank you, dearest sweetheart.

Melanie got married seven months after Trudi died. She invited me to her dress fitting. I went because I wanted to get my crying over with, seeing her in a wedding dress. Afterwards, we went out to lunch and she asked me to give a talk at the reception, I took notes during lunch. My goal for the speech was to delicately balance the joy of the wedding with the sadness of not having her mother.

It was a great wedding. I gave the speech. And we had a wonderful reception. There was one snag, though. At about 10:30 in the evening, the lights went out. There was a lot of talk about the McMullens' resiliency because we never missed a beat! The band played on under candlelight.

It wasn't until the next day, while putting away my wedding file, I came across the notes I took the day of Melanie's dress fitting. I had forgotten I had them. I called Melanie to remind her what she had told me according to my notes. Melanie had wanted a sign that her mother was with her – like a tapping on the ceiling, or lights flickering. Instead the whole grid surrounding the Women's Club lost electricity! Trudi never did things half way.

Melissa got married two months after Melanie. She wanted to get married at her mother's house. She had movers come and take out all the furniture. Then she prepared the house for a wedding and a party – tables and chairs and a dance floor were delivered. It was quite a touching event. Melissa and Todd's son, Trudan, named after Trudi, had already been born. I was particularly moved by the comfort that Melissa felt by being at her mom's house. The next day the house was emptied and the cleaners came. And the day after that all the furniture was returned. I woke up the next morning and thought, "Did we really have Melissa's wedding here, or did just I dream it?"

People have asked Pat, "What's it like being married to Tom who was married to a woman as strong as Trudi?" Pat graciously replies, "I embrace Trudi. We would have been good friends. I would have loved her. I feel so privileged to be surrounded by such goodness."

The first Christmas after we were married, Pat was going through all the decorations stored in the basement when she was struck by the overwhelming presence of Trudi. She said she felt Trudi watching her go through things. Pat cried and told her that she would take care of her grandchildren and love them.

She also felt this strong presence the first time she took Melissa's two boys out with her. A cardinal landed in the low branch of a tree, right in front of Pat as she was walking with the boys out the front door. Pat felt inspired by that special moment.

Another example of the impact that a cardinal has had in our lives happened on our return flight from Jacksonville, FL. There was a couple with two young children. She sat across the aisle from us with one child and he sat behind us with the other. We became friends during the flight, got to know their names, a little family history, and Pat helped distract their one-year-old by holding her.

When we deplaned, we helped them carry some luggage, as their hands were full. When we got to the terminal, the young boy, probably almost three years old, said to his mother, "I see the cardinal." The mother got down to his level and looked him in the eyes and said, "Isn't it nice that you feel Maxwell's presence, and that he's keeping you safe." I looked at her and said, "Do you have a son in heaven?" She said "yes," and that their family sees a cardinal as a sign that Maxwell and the Holy Spirit are in their lives. She also said that in his honor, they commemorated a bench at Lake Harriet near the band shell. Pat and I then left and headed our own way.

A couple of months later, Pat was walking at Lake Harriet with her daughter, Laura, and decided to try to find the bench. She did, and told me about it that night. Later that summer, Pat and I had dinner at Tin Fish on Lake Calhoun. As we were leaving I said, "I want to go over to Harriet and find that bench." When we got close we realized there was a concert at the band shell and the place was packed. Just as we got to the spot where

Pat thought the bench was, a car pulled out of their parking spot and Pat and I pulled in. She said, "I think it's one of those two benches." There was a young couple in their mid- to late-twenties sitting on the first bench so I circled around to come up to them from the front, rather than coming up behind them and startling them. I told them what I was looking for and sure enough, there was the plaque with Maxwell's name: Maxwell Douglas Adamek Best. They got up, made a couple comments, and then she leaned over to read the plaque.

"What's going on here?" she said in a loud troubled voice. "You walk up here with a story of meeting someone on a plane to see if this is their little boy's bench and...that's my name. My name is Adamek. I've never been here before. I'm from St. Paul." "And your grandfather was from St. Cloud," I said, having learned that on our plane ride. The Adamek family moved from St. Cloud, some went to Minneapolis and some went to St. Paul, and evidently they lost touch with each other. The young lady was still in shock. "I'm related to this boy – I don't know what to think. What do you suppose this means?" I said, "I don't know what it means to you, but I do know what it means to me." And with that, I hurriedly left. I do have a regret that I didn't stay and talk with them. What I wish I would have said is that our "chance" meeting is another powerful example of how the Holy Spirit is working in my life, and I suspect all of our lives, helping us see how we're all connected. And I would have added that I know there's more to our lives than what we can see.

Step 11

*"Sought through prayer and mediation
to improve our conscious contact with
God, as we understood Him, praying
only for knowledge of His will for us
and the power to carry that out."*

Dick Lund

What Came to Me

*Thirty-six years ago I first made this decision
After I came to believe, but only in my head.
I had to wait awhile for God to reach my heart,
I kept the door open, had to, else I'd be dead.*

Why did I wait? I dunno.
God's work is a mystery, so I just listened,
And I prayed, and I prayed and I prayed.
For what was missing.

One night I heard Doug say, "God within."
And later I heard Ted say, "Care of God."
Tom said, "God is a feeling."
God is love came from, "As we understood Him."

God was the only way I could continue to live
I heard I had a God-sized hole in my soul
Happily, I was ready to fill it,
The feeling of love within, a visitation of grace.

I see life now with divine light of love,
I am lovable, I am loved, I am loving. I'm God's creation.
I have been made whole.
A visitation of grace, a transformation.

As saint I've yet no honor in my house.
Because, she says, the smug in me still shows.
As all of you add wisdom, like my spouse.
I'll use to find the joys avoid the woes.

TOM MCMULLEN

I started kindergarten at Bancroft Public School when I was four. My mother drove me to school and dropped me off. Three or four years before she died, she said to me: "Tommy, there's something I have to apologize for. I dropped you off at kindergarten on your first day and said, 'You go in that door.' I never gave it two thoughts that you might be frightened." She had her hands full with all the kids, what did she know? I was terrified! I went in crying and my older sister Mary Kay, who was enrolled at Holy Name (a few blocks away), had to be pulled out of her school to come to Bancroft to help me. She switched schools and spent first grade at Bancroft because I wouldn't stay unless she was in the school. Mary Kay and I walked to school together every day and she would stay in my class until I settled down. She spent a year there helping me. That summer, when she was six, she broke her ankle. I pulled her around in my wagon, and helped her hobble around during the whole summer.

Mary Kay had five boys. Her middle son, Timmy, had been an alcoholic since he was a teenager. He lived on the streets of Minneapolis for 20 years. Mary Kay had done a lot of praying for Timmy to live a sober life. She prayed for him to be safe from the terrible beatings that he'd been through, and the other pain that a homeless alcoholic experiences. After years of watching him live in pain, her prayers changed to those of wanting Timmy to have a peaceful death. She got the call that said, "Your son, Tim, has been found dead." The next day, Mary Kay and I went to where he was found. Across the alley was a health care facility where the boys who found Timmy ran in to tell Jackie. We found Jackie and she and Mary Kay held each other and cried. Jackie didn't know if there was anyone who loved Timmy. She volunteered to Mary Kay, "I want you to know that your son died a peaceful death."

I gave the eulogy at a packed St. Olaf Church, Downtown Minneapolis. Mary Kay asked me to help make sense of Timmy's life. She worked across the street at the Government Center. Her job was the information booth, where all the people who were headed to court came to ask directions on how to get to their courtrooms. On occasion, Timmy would come in, perhaps drunk, and she would have to ask him to leave. Mary Kay was such was an inspiration to everyone she met – she imparted the Holy Spirit to all she met – her nickname was, "Mother Hennepin." Basically, the government center walked across the street to the funeral that morning.

When I started the eulogy, I looked out in the front row and saw my four sisters with their eyes just glued on me, wondering what I was going to say. I opened the eulogy with, "There are my four sisters in the front row, staring at me. It reminds me a little bit of the bumper sticker I saw that reads, 'Lord help me become the kind of person my dog thinks I am." I've had that with my sisters all my life. They've just expected good things from me. They've been an inspiration for me to be better than I really am.

Timmy's high school girlfriend came and invited her friend, Anne, to come with her. Anne was a reporter for the *Star & Tribune* newspaper. Moved by what she saw and heard that day, she wrote an article titled, "A Life Taken Drop By Drop, " which was published on the front page. Mary Kay got calls and letters from all over the world. "We have a Timmy," so many would say. And then she'd do what she's done for so much of her life – bless them with her hope and peace. There is such irony in how Timmy lived his life. He never recovered from alcoholism; lived and ultimately died on the streets. And yet, he has had a timeless impact on so many.

Previously, when I was 25 and Melissa was about a year old, I told Trudi that when we got back from New York (we had been away on business), I was going to call AA. Trudi thought I was nuts! She told me just not to drink so much, that I wasn't an alcoholic. This was in 1967. I had been told by many people that I was an alcoholic, and I had seen alcoholism in my Uncle Raymond, who everybody said I was just like. The guys came to my house and gave me a test; I failed, so I started going to AA meetings. I went for about seven months, and drank once in between. I was called "the kid" since I was so young compared to the other people in the group. One day, I "realized" that I had a lot of good drinking years left. So I announced to the group that starting next week, I was going back to drinking and no longer coming to meetings. Knowing there was nothing they could do or say to stop me, they told me that it was probably a good idea, but that they expected to see me again.

My drinking started getting bad at that point. I tried to control it but couldn't and had a lot of negative things happen. Like fights with Trudi. Fights with others at bars. Spending money I didn't have. Writing bad checks.

Thanksgiving of 1969 we spent at Trudi's grandparents'. They were good Lutherans from a small town. They passed around a little tray of two-ounce cups of wine. But when it came to me I knew I had to pass because I knew that if I drank that two ounces, I would be banging on doors all over town looking for anyone with a jug of whiskey. I realized that day just how compulsive alcohol was for me.

I was unemployed at the time. I had just quit working for my father in September, had lost our health insurance, the company car, and was driving Trudi's poorly running Corvair.

The coming Christmas season turned out to be the most painful time of my life. My daughter Melanie was born on December 11 that year. Three days earlier, I had started a new job with McCulloch Industries. I was drinking virtually full time. My attention span was so short, my cognitive abilities were so poor, that I couldn't write a sentence. I couldn't remember a phone call or take an order at work. It got extremely stressful for me with this new job. And now I had two little daughters. Trudi was upset by my drinking, and upset at not having any money. We were so broke that season that one time I put my bankcard in the ATM and it gave me $20. I thought there had to have been a mistake because I didn't have $20.

My daughter Melissa, who was less than three at the time, still to this day remembers my drinking. She remembers standing at the top of the stairs and pleading, "Papa please don't go. Papa please don't go." Of course, I had to go out anyway and just drink.

Then, a life altering set of circumstances came together and I went to a different AA meeting on New Year's Eve that same year. It was my 27th birthday. I drank again on January 12th and that is my most vivid memory of drinking. I was so drunk that I tried to run a semi off the road. I remember the semi hitting the guardrail and screeching down the highway. He finally got control of his vehicle and he laid on the horn. I got off on France Avenue and he went under the bridge and laid on the horn all the way up I-494. I can still hear it! He should have killed me, run right over that tiny Corvair, but he didn't. That last Christmas season was the most painful time of my life, and the last time I drank. January 13th is my sobriety date.

There were a lot of events that led to me quitting drinking but Melanie's birth the most significant. At my first AA meeting there was a man by the name of Redman. I got so much out of what he had said, I came back the next week and asked where he was. They said that he had killed himself because he went back to drinking and couldn't take it anymore. This also happened with Conrad and Roy. The AA men were very clear with me. They said, "You have a disease and it's called alcoholism. You can have a premature death, or have happiness and a great life, whatever you choose. All you have to do is not drink and come to meetings. You're the luckiest guy in the world if you know that."

Step 12

"Having had a spiritual
awakening as the result of
these Steps, we tried to carry
this message to alcoholics,
and to practice these
principles in all our affairs."

Dick Lund

A Meditation

Awake? Yes! I'm aroused! By God's sweet grace,
A mystery, yes, but one that I embrace.

Just when did that occur, I ask? And how?
A tale to tell of others I avow.

Awakened? It is I, but who am I?
A question I can't ask without a sigh.
Medallion says, "To thine own self be true."
Who is this self I must create anew?

Existence? Being? Creature? Spirit? Soul?
Perhaps a bit of each. A lump of coal?
The way is truth and practice without sham.
In time I'll surely know just who I am.

"Carry the message," is telling the tale,
A message to heal, or get out of jail,
The message we hear, the message we tell,
A wondrous exchange of making us well.

The tale is told by some of life set free,
And others, too, of joy and long-sought glee,
I hear a word, a phrase that stirs my soul,
Enough for me to say it makes me whole.

I've learned to love myself whoe're I be,
And learned to love all others now I see.
The Holy Spirit's work of every kind,
I pray each day to always keep in mind.

TOM MCMULLEN

I've always said the only thing I've ever accomplished in my life is working the AA program. I've been able to let it seep in week after week, slowly. When we first went to the Johnson Institute, Trudi couldn't think of one good thing about me. But at her death, with her last breath, she said, "Tom." Can you imagine the gratitude I feel having taken this journey with Trudi. Trudi said to me, "How is it possible that you have changed so much?" I said, "Well, you've seen me go to meetings." She replied, "No, I've seen a lot of people go to meetings, but you, your entire nature, has changed."

All of my life I had been in the habit of re-doing mistakes. I think this was because my normal feelings were pressure, pain, anger and fear. Whenever something good would happen, being uncomfortable with this feeling, I would do something to bring back my "normal" feelings. So many people are dealing with this same thing.

And now I'm different! How did this happen? What did I do to change? I think a lot of it has to do with how willing I was to keep on trying. All the self-help books I've read, all the seminars I've been to, all the listening I've done when someone has a piece of what I want, all the trial and error... I also believe that I've been offered a gift by God. My only job has been to accept this gift, be thankful, and do my best to let it develop.

It came together for me: I was home alone and walked by the four-foot mirror in the hallway. I looked into it for probably the thousandth time, only this time it was different. This time, I only looked into my eyes. I think it was probably a six- to eight-minute experience. I stared in amazement at the profound feeling of love and acceptance I had for myself. I talked to that guy behind those eyes. I told him I understand what he had been through. I knew how hard he had worked, how willing he was to feel different, and how much I loved him. I put my arms around myself, rubbed my shoulders, and accepted myself 100% for the first time in my life. I invited the pain to leave and said, "thank you." I was transformed in those moments. For weeks, every time I walked by that mirror, I stood and looked into my eyes, the feelings were profound. Try it! Don't look at the wrinkles, or the pimple, or the nose that isn't perfect, or the receding hairline – just stare into your eyes. If you're like me, tears will begin to flow and your acceptance of yourself will rise to a new level. Life for me would never be the same after that experience. I love the saying, "If you know you're evolving, you can evolve even faster." I'm often in awe of what's happened to me.

Changes

New Years, twenty-fourteen, a prophesy,
    Emphasize the new, change, whatever you want to be.
Transformation, attitude and outlook,
    A time for resolution, time to see.

Time to give yourself space, what do you want?
    Change in doing or change in your seeing?
Or just awareness of what you have lost,
    No sense of center, no ground of being?

Masks we wear, false masks our self to protect,
    Is one content in a crowd such as this?
The quest for true self, for truth, enters in,
    Truth lies within. Could it be? Find your bliss.

New self, new you, but misapprehension,
    "How" is the question, the answer's "intention."
Connection with true self, lost from the start.
    Truth overtakes us, God's the connection.

All of us need a little outside help,
    Prayer and presence of one gentle friend,
To live a new life and be a new self,
    Give self permission, for life on the mend.

— Dick Lund

Epilogue

There you have it. The stories of two friends, who resurrect our lives out of grief and disorder brought on by the affliction of alcoholism. We suffered the same turmoil of youth and early adulthood and with outside help are recovering from alcoholism. In the course of recovery, by serendipity, our paths crossed, we became fast friends, and were both taken with desire to "pay it forward" by writing this book.

To those who are still suffering with their addiction:

The disease is in control of your life. Do what you have to do to get well. Trust that someone beside you can help. Tell a friend just how bad it is for you. This might be the only moment when you have clarity regarding your illness. Put yourself in someone else's hands and trust that it will start you on a wonderful journey.

To the loved ones of someone suffering from addiction:

The disease is in control of your loved one's life. You, and those close to you, have slowly let the disease infect your lives, as well. You need help to stop the process. Reach out to someone and ask for help. This may be the only moment of clarity when you can see what you need. Do something now. You don't have to reach bottom, where lives are destroyed. The bottom for you, and the addicted, can be created at a higher level. You need outside help to make this happen and trust that all will be well.

Resurrect!

ACKNOWLEDGEMENT

A Little Outside Help

A major theme in living a life of recovery from addiction is outside help; we can't do it on our own. So it is too, in telling our tale. We couldn't have brought this book to fruition without the invaluable help of three women in particular, our friends: Jennifer Miller of Strengths Way; Deirdre Thompson of WinsomeCreative.biz; and Catherine Plessner, one of Tom's four sisters. These three, whom we have dubbed our "Brain Trust," inspired us to ever keep in mind the universal maxim, "no man is an island."

Appendix A

Dick's Recommended Reading, The Short List

Alcoholics Anonymous
Twelve Steps and Twelve Traditions
Road less Traveled–M. Scott Peck (and many others)
Mere Christianity–C.S. Lewis
Screwtape Letters–C. S. Lewis
Varieties of Religious Experience – William James
Modern Man in Search of a Soul – Carl Jung
Memories Dreams and Reflections – Carl Jung
Dialogs of Plato
Contemplative Prayer–Thomas Merton (and his many other works)
The Power of Now–Eckhart Tolle (and his others)
Mysticism–Evelyn Underhill
Ultimate Concern–Paul Tillich (and his others)

Mystics and Zen Masters – Thomas Merton

Essays in Zen Buddhism–D.T. Suzuki

Ethics — Aristotle

Essays–Ralph Waldo Emerson

The Case for God–Karen Armstrong

The Rule of St. Benedict–Anthony Meisel

The Three Pillars of Zen–D. T. Suzuki

The Art of Thinking–Ernest Dimnet

Dark Night of the Soul–St. John of the Cross

The Cloud of Unknowing–Anonymous

Wisdom of the Desert – Thomas Merton

Basic Writings of Carl Jung

The Great Thoughts–George Seldes

Benedict's Way–Lonnie Pratt and Father Daniel Homan, OSB

Undiscovered Self – Carl Jung

World's Religions–Huston Smith

Mind Whispering–Tara Bennett–Goleman

Mindsight–Dr. Daniel Siegel

Care of the Soul–Thomas More

Dakota–Kathleen Norris

The Case for God–Karen Armstrong

Imitation of Christ–Thomas á Kempis

A Common Faith–John Dewey

Appendix B

Tom's Frequent &
Inspirational Sayings

I'll see it when I believe it. – *Wayne Dyer*

A fluke is one of God's best moves.

When you change the way you look at things, the things you look at change. – *Wayne Dyer*

Face your negatives early.

I feel good, I feel God.

If you knew who walked beside you at all times, on the path that you have chosen, you could never experience fear or doubt again. – *Wayne Dyer*

I am open to God's presence within me.

I feel God's presence in my daily life and know that I am one with God. All of my blessings flow from this knowing.

My attention is focused on abundance and on moving forward.

I attract abundance, prosperity and greatness into my life, and pass this on to others as I go through my day.

I know that my day is going to be filled with many absolute wonderful, miraculous, spirit guided occurrences.

Because I am supremely focused on the present moment, the right response comes to me in every situation as it occurs.

I choose the images to which I give my attention and energy.

Commitment is never an act of moderation. – *Kenneth Mills*

The moment I commit, dormant forces come alive to help me. Things line up almost magically in my favor.

My needs are met with ease and grace.

I don't mind what happens.

I feel ...peace, passion, love, energy, zestful, purposeful, inspired, hopeful, trust, alive, prosperous, free, honest, compassion, happy, abundance, willing, strong, healthy, gratitude, serenity, good, God.

At day's end, and often during the day, I thank God for all my blessings.

I always have time for everything; it's the darndest thing.

I have so much help beyond myself.

To me, God is a feeling.

If you want to make God laugh, tell him your plans. – *Woody Allen*

All my life is a prayer.

Does it need to be said? Does it need to be said by me? Does it need to be said right now? – *Craig Ferguson and Nick*

You can't solve a problem with the same mind that created it. – *Eckhart Tolle*

BETTER TOGETHER

Friends Resurrect

Made in the USA
San Bernardino, CA
25 May 2014